G000123786

DREAM
BELIEVE
ACHIEVE

summersdale

DREAM, BELIEVE, ACHIEVE

An Hachette UK Company
www.hachette.co.uk

Summersdale Publishers Ltd
Part of Octopus Publishing Group Limited
Carmelite House
50 Victoria Embankment
LONDON
EC4Y 0DZ
UK

www.summersdale.com

Printed and bound in China

ISBN: 978-1-78783-689-1

Substantial discounts on bulk quantities of Summersdale books are available to corporations, professional associations and other organizations. For details contact general enquiries: telephone: +44 (0) 1243 771107 or email: enquiries@summersdale.com.

TO.....................................

FROM..................................

One of the most important things you can accomplish is just being yourself.

DWAYNE JOHNSON

SUCCESS IS SIMPLE.
DO WHAT'S RIGHT,
THE RIGHT WAY,
AT THE RIGHT TIME.

ARNOLD H. GLASOW

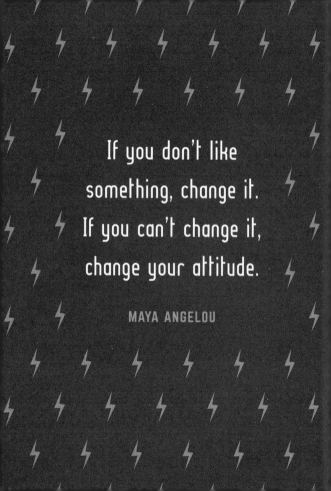

If you don't like something, change it. If you can't change it, change your attitude.

MAYA ANGELOU

However bad life may seem,
there is always something
you can do, and succeed at.

STEPHEN HAWKING

**SUCCESS IS NOT FINAL,
FAILURE IS NOT FATAL:
IT IS THE COURAGE TO
CONTINUE THAT COUNTS.**

ANONYMOUS

LIVE DARINGLY, BOLDLY,
FEARLESSLY. TASTE THE
RELISH TO BE FOUND
IN COMPETITION –
IN HAVING PUT FORTH
THE BEST WITHIN YOU.

HENRY J. KAISER

DON'T BE AFRAID
TO GIVE UP THE GOOD
TO GO FOR THE GREAT.

JOHN D. ROCKEFELLER

KNOW YOURSELF TO BETTER YOURSELF

I LEARNED TO ALWAYS
TAKE ON THINGS I'D
NEVER DONE BEFORE.
GROWTH AND COMFORT
DO NOT COEXIST.

GINNI ROMETTY

**ACTION IS THE
FOUNDATIONAL KEY
TO ALL SUCCESS.**

PABLO PICASSO

Be sure what you
want and be sure
about yourself...
You have to believe
in yourself and
be strong.

ADRIANA LIMA

THE QUESTION ISN'T
WHO IS GOING TO LET ME;
IT'S WHO IS GOING
TO STOP ME.

AYN RAND

Only those
who dare to fail
greatly can ever
achieve greatly.

ROBERT F. KENNEDY

Your self-worth is
determined by you.
You don't have to depend
on someone telling you
who you are.

BEYONCÉ

**SUCCESSFUL PEOPLE DO
WHAT UNSUCCESSFUL PEOPLE
ARE NOT WILLING TO DO.
DON'T WISH IT WERE EASIER;
WISH YOU WERE BETTER.**

JIM ROHN

MANY OF LIFE'S
FAILURES ARE PEOPLE
WHO DID NOT REALIZE
HOW CLOSE THEY WERE
TO SUCCESS WHEN
THEY GAVE UP.

THOMAS EDISON

IT'S ALWAYS TOO EARLY TO QUIT.

NORMAN VINCENT PEALE

Pearls don't lie on the seashore – if you want one, you have to dive for it

WHEN WE OWN
THE STORY, WE
CAN WRITE A BRAVE
NEW ENDING.

BRENÉ BROWN

**EXPECT PROBLEMS
AND EAT THEM
FOR BREAKFAST.**

ALFRED A.
MONTAPERT

You are perfectly
cast in your life.
I can't imagine
anyone but you
in the role.

LIN-MANUEL MIRANDA

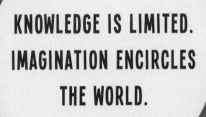

KNOWLEDGE IS LIMITED.
IMAGINATION ENCIRCLES
THE WORLD.

ALBERT EINSTEIN

You are not
your résumé; you
are your work.

SETH GODIN

Take criticism seriously,
but not personally.

HILLARY CLINTON

THE MOST EFFECTIVE
WAY TO DO IT
IS TO DO IT.

AMELIA EARHART

DEVELOP SUCCESS
FROM FAILURES.
DISCOURAGEMENT AND
FAILURE ARE TWO OF
THE SUREST STEPPING
STONES TO SUCCESS.

DALE CARNEGIE

TO CONQUER
WITHOUT RISK
IS TO TRIUMPH
WITHOUT GLORY.

PIERRE CORNEILLE

Dreams
DON'T WORK
unless
YOU DO

THE MOST COMMON
WAY PEOPLE GIVE UP
THEIR POWER IS BY
THINKING THEY
DON'T HAVE ANY.

ALICE WALKER

TO LEARN PATIENCE
IS NOT TO REBEL
AGAINST EVERY
HARDSHIP.

HENRI NOUWEN

The important thing
is not being afraid
to take a chance.
Remember, the
greatest failure
is to not try.

DEBBI FIELDS

IF ANYTHING IS
WORTH DOING, DO IT WITH
ALL YOUR HEART.

BUDDHA

The future belongs
to those who believe
in the beauty of
their dreams.

ANONYMOUS

I didn't get there by wishing for it or hoping for it, but by working for it.

ESTÉE LAUDER

ACT AS IF WHAT
YOU DO MAKES
A DIFFERENCE.
IT DOES.

WILLIAM JAMES

I'M NOT GOING TO LIMIT
MYSELF JUST BECAUSE
PEOPLE WON'T ACCEPT
THE FACT THAT I CAN DO
SOMETHING ELSE.

DOLLY PARTON

THERE IS NO EDUCATION LIKE ADVERSITY.

BENJAMIN DISRAELI

Hope is
the heartbeat
of the soul

CHANGE YOUR
LIFE TODAY. DON'T
GAMBLE ON THE
FUTURE, ACT NOW,
WITHOUT DELAY.

SIMONE DE BEAUVOIR

WHATEVER THE MIND OF MAN CAN CONCEIVE AND BELIEVE, IT CAN ACHIEVE.

NAPOLEON HILL

If you're walking down the right path and you're willing to keep walking, eventually you'll make progress.

BARACK OBAMA

I ALWAYS DID
SOMETHING I WAS
A LITTLE NOT
READY TO DO.

MARISSA MAYER

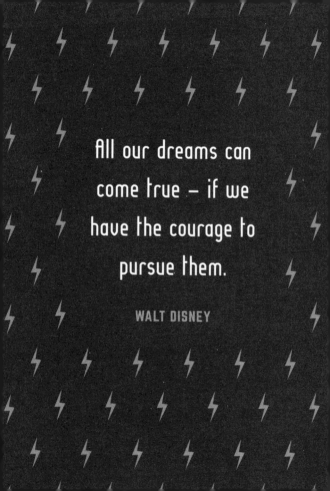

All our dreams can come true — if we have the courage to pursue them.

WALT DISNEY

Start where you are.
Use what you have.
Do what you can.

ARTHUR ASHE

YOU ONLY HAVE TO DO A VERY FEW THINGS RIGHT... SO LONG AS YOU DON'T DO TOO MANY THINGS WRONG.

WARREN BUFFETT

⚡

DEFINE SUCCESS ON
YOUR OWN TERMS,
ACHIEVE IT BY YOUR
OWN RULES, AND
BUILD A LIFE YOU'RE
PROUD TO LIVE.

ANNE SWEENEY

THE ONLY PLACE
WHERE SUCCESS COMES
BEFORE WORK IS IN
THE DICTIONARY.

VIDAL SASSOON

THERE IS NO ELEVATOR TO SUCCESS; YOU HAVE TO TAKE THE STAIRS

ENTREPRENEURS
AVERAGE 3.8 FAILURES
BEFORE FINAL SUCCESS.
WHAT SETS THE
SUCCESSFUL ONES
APART IS THEIR
AMAZING PERSISTENCE.

LISA M. AMOS

STOP CHASING
THE MONEY AND
START CHASING
THE PASSION.

TONY HSIEH

Every worthwhile
accomplishment,
big or little, has its
stages of drudgery
and triumph:
a beginning,
a struggle
and a victory.

MAHATMA GANDHI

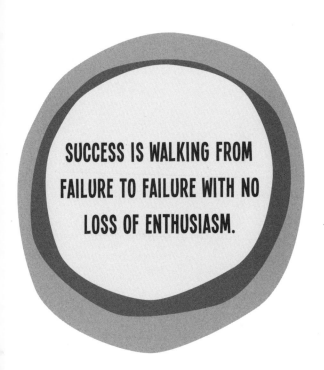

SUCCESS IS WALKING FROM FAILURE TO FAILURE WITH NO LOSS OF ENTHUSIASM.

ANONYMOUS

Opportunities
don't happen,
you create them.

CHRIS GROSSER

Feet, what do I need them
for if I have wings to fly.

FRIDA KAHLO

NEVER GIVE UP THEN,
FOR THAT'S JUST THE
PLACE AND TIME THAT
THE TIDE'LL TURN.

HARRIET
BEECHER STOWE

WOULD YOU LIKE ME
GIVE YOU A FORMULA
FOR SUCCESS? IT'S QUITE
SIMPLE, REALLY. DOUBLE
YOUR RATE OF FAILURE.

THOMAS J. WATSON

THE ONE WHO FALLS AND GETS UP IS STRONGER THAN THE ONE WHO NEVER TRIED.

ROY T. BENNETT

DARE
TO
DREAM

PEOPLE MAY HEAR YOUR
WORDS, BUT THEY FEEL
YOUR ATTITUDE.

JOHN C. MAXWELL

THE BEST WAY TO PREDICT THE FUTURE IS TO INVENT IT.

ALAN KAY

If you're offered
a seat on a rocket
ship, don't ask
what seat.

SHERYL SANDBERG

WHEN THE
WHOLE WORLD IS
SILENT, EVEN ONE VOICE
BECOMES POWERFUL.

MALALA YOUSAFZAI

There is no dream
that's too big.

LADY GAGA

The difference between successful people and others is how long they spend time feeling sorry for themselves.

BARBARA CORCORAN

YOU CAN NEVER LEAVE FOOTPRINTS THAT LAST IF YOU ARE ALWAYS WALKING ON TIPTOE.

LEYMAH GBOWEE

BELIEF IN ONESELF
IS ONE OF THE MOST
IMPORTANT BRICKS
IN BUILDING ANY
SUCCESSFUL VENTURE.

LYDIA MARIA CHILD

IF YOU REALLY
LOOK CLOSELY, MOST
OVERNIGHT SUCCESSES
TOOK A LONG TIME.

STEVE JOBS

Do something today that your future self will thank you for

IT'S NEVER TOO LATE
TO TAKE A LEAP OF FAITH
AND SEE WHAT WILL
HAPPEN – AND TO BE
BRAVE IN LIFE.

JANE FONDA

A DREAM DOESN'T
BECOME REALITY
THROUGH MAGIC;
IT TAKES SWEAT,
DETERMINATION
AND HARD WORK.

COLIN POWELL

To accomplish
great things we
must not only act,
but also dream;
not only plan,
but also believe.

ANATOLE FRANCE

I WAS SMART ENOUGH
TO GO THROUGH ANY
DOOR THAT OPENED.

JOAN RIVERS

If you wait,
all that happens
is that you
get older.

MARIO ANDRETTI

It's more important to stand for something. If you don't stand for something, what do you win?

LANE KIRKLAND

IF YOU CAN FIND
A PATH WITH NO
OBSTACLES, IT PROBABLY
DOESN'T LEAD ANYWHERE.

FRANK A. CLARK

ONLY THROUGH
EXPERIENCE OF TRIAL
AND SUFFERING CAN THE
SOUL BE STRENGTHENED,
VISION CLEARED,
AMBITION INSPIRED,
AND SUCCESS ACHIEVED.

HELEN KELLER

THERE IS AN OLD SAYING THAT THINGS DON'T HAPPEN, THEY ARE MADE TO HAPPEN.

JOHN F. KENNEDY

Every day
IS ANOTHER
chance to
MAKE A CHANGE

⚡

IF YOU DON'T
GET OUT THERE AND
DEFINE YOURSELF,
YOU'LL BE QUICKLY
AND INACCURATELY
DEFINED BY OTHERS.

MICHELLE OBAMA

ACCEPT THE CHALLENGES, SO THAT YOU MAY FEEL THE EXHILARATION OF VICTORY.

GEORGE S. PATTON

Being defeated is often a temporary condition. Giving up is what makes it permanent.

MARILYN vos SAVANT

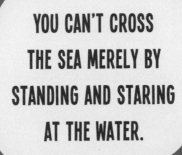

YOU CAN'T CROSS
THE SEA MERELY BY
STANDING AND STARING
AT THE WATER.

RABINDRANATH TAGORE

Shoot for the moon.
Even if you miss,
you'll land among
the stars.

LES BROWN

Instead of wondering when your next vacation is, you ought to set up a life you don't need to escape from.

SETH GODIN

WE MAY ENCOUNTER
MANY DEFEATS,
BUT WE MUST
NOT BE DEFEATED.

MAYA ANGELOU

THROW CAUTION
TO THE WIND
AND JUST DO IT.

NIAMH GREENE

IF YOU WANT SOMETHING NEW, YOU HAVE TO STOP DOING SOMETHING OLD.

PETER F. DRUCKER

BE
STUBBORN
ABOUT
YOUR
GOALS AND
FLEXIBLE
ABOUT
YOUR
METHODS

YOU CAN GO
AS FAR AS YOUR
MIND LETS YOU.
WHAT YOU BELIEVE,
REMEMBER, YOU
CAN ACHIEVE.

MARY KAY ASH

KEEP YOUR EYES ON
THE STARS, BUT REMEMBER
TO KEEP YOUR FEET
ON THE GROUND.

THEODORE
ROOSEVELT

Success is a
state of mind.
If you want
success, start
thinking of
yourself as
a success.

JOYCE BROTHERS

IF YOU DON'T LIKE
THE ROAD YOU'RE
WALKING, START PAVING
ANOTHER ONE.

DOLLY PARTON

One fails forward
toward success.

CHARLES KETTERING

Being negative only makes
a difficult journey more
difficult. You may be given
a cactus, but you don't
have to sit on it.

JOYCE MEYER

KNOWING IS NOT ENOUGH;
WE MUST APPLY.
WILLING IS NOT ENOUGH;
WE MUST DO.

JOHANN. WOLFGANG
VON GOETHE

LET ME TELL YOU THE
SECRET THAT HAS LED
ME TO MY GOAL. MY
STRENGTH LIES SOLELY
IN MY TENACITY.

LOUIS PASTEUR

THE SECRET OF GETTING AHEAD IS GETTING STARTED.

ANONYMOUS

*Life is a
one-time offer –
use it wisely*

A LOT OF PEOPLE ARE
AFRAID TO SAY WHAT
THEY WANT. THAT'S WHY
THEY DON'T GET WHAT
THEY WANT.

MADONNA

WHEN WE STRIVE TO
BECOME BETTER THAN WE
ARE, EVERYTHING AROUND
US BECOMES BETTER TOO.

PAULO COELHO

Sometimes you can't see yourself clearly until you see yourself through the eyes of others.

ELLEN DeGENERES

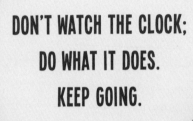

DON'T WATCH THE CLOCK;
DO WHAT IT DOES.
KEEP GOING.

SAM LEVENSON

Live as if you were
to die tomorrow.
Learn as if you were
to live forever.

MAHATMA GANDHI.

We know what we are, but know not what we may be.

WILLIAM SHAKESPEARE

OPPORTUNITIES
MULTIPLY AS
THEY ARE SEIZED.

SUN TZU

THE ONLY WAY OF
DISCOVERING THE LIMITS
OF THE POSSIBLE IS
TO VENTURE A LITTLE
WAY PAST THEM INTO
THE IMPOSSIBLE.

ARTHUR C. CLARKE

WE ARE THE CHANGE THAT WE SEEK.

BARACK OBAMA

HARD
WORK
PAYS
OFF

YOUR PRESENT
CIRCUMSTANCES DON'T
DETERMINE WHERE
YOU CAN GO; THEY
MERELY DETERMINE
WHERE YOU START.

NIDO QUBEIN

DON'T WORRY ABOUT
PEOPLE STEALING AN IDEA.
IF IT'S ORIGINAL, YOU WILL
HAVE TO RAM IT DOWN
THEIR THROATS.

HOWARD H. AIKEN

Success seems to be connected with action. Successful people keep moving. They make mistakes, but they don't quit.

CONRAD HILTON

IF YOU SEE A
BANDWAGON,
IT'S TOO LATE.

JAMES GOLDSMITH

Every great
dream begins
with a dreamer.

ANONYMOUS

The only limit
to our realization
of tomorrow will be
our doubts of today.

FRANKLIN D. ROOSEVELT

WHEN SOMETHING IS
IMPORTANT ENOUGH,
YOU DO IT EVEN IF
THE ODDS ARE NOT
IN YOUR FAVOUR.

ELON MUSK

I'M A SERIOUS OPTIMIST.
I COME FROM A COUNTRY
WHERE YOU HAVE LITTLE
TO BE HOPEFUL FOR, AND
SO YOU HAVE TO ALWAYS
BE AN OPTIMIST.

LEYMAH GBOWEE

LIFE CHANGES VERY QUICKLY, IN A VERY POSITIVE WAY, IF YOU LET IT.

LINDSEY VONN

Never let your fear decide your future

IF YOU REALLY WANT TO
DO SOMETHING, YOU'LL
FIND A WAY. IF YOU DON'T,
YOU'LL FIND AN EXCUSE.

JIM ROHN

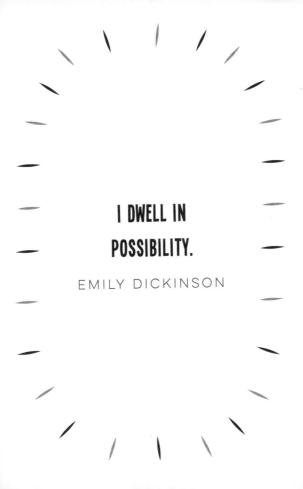

I DWELL IN
POSSIBILITY.

EMILY DICKINSON

Winners take time
to relish their work,
knowing that scaling
the mountain is what
makes the view from
the top so exhilarating.

DENIS WAITLEY

YOU ARE NEVER
TOO OLD TO SET
ANOTHER GOAL OR TO
DREAM A NEW DREAM.

LES BROWN

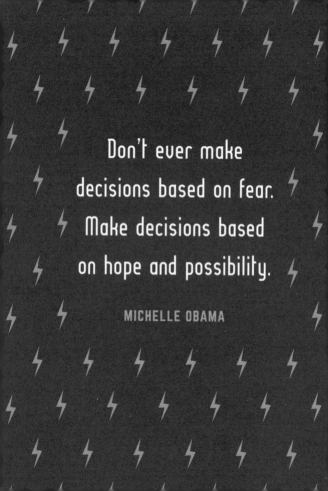

Don't ever make decisions based on fear. Make decisions based on hope and possibility.

MICHELLE OBAMA

The only person you are destined to become is the person you decide to be.

RALPH WALDO EMERSON

**DON'T JUDGE EACH
DAY BY THE HARVEST YOU
REAP BUT BY THE SEEDS
THAT YOU PLANT.**

ROBERT LOUIS
STEVENSON

YOU SHOULDN'T GO
THROUGH LIFE WITH
A CATCHER'S MITT ON
BOTH HANDS; YOU NEED
TO BE ABLE TO THROW
SOMETHING BACK.

MAYA ANGELOU

CONTROL YOUR DESTINY OR SOMEONE ELSE WILL.

JACK WELCH

One positive
THOUGHT CAN
change your
WHOLE DAY

HAPPINESS IS THE KEY
TO SUCCESS. IF YOU
LOVE WHAT YOU ARE
DOING, YOU WILL BE
SUCCESSFUL.

ALBERT SCHWEITZER

**INNOVATION
DISTINGUISHES
BETWEEN
A LEADER AND
A FOLLOWER.**

STEVE JOBS

To the degree
we're not living
our dreams,
our comfort zone
has more control
of us than we have
over ourselves.

PETER McWILLIAMS

IT TAKES COURAGE
TO GROW UP AND TURN
OUT TO BE WHO YOU
REALLY ARE.

E. E. CUMMINGS

It is better to fail in originality, than to succeed in imitation.

HERMAN MELVILLE

Hard work and ambition
can take you a long way.

DWAYNE JOHNSON

SUCCESS USUALLY COMES TO THOSE WHO ARE TOO BUSY TO BE LOOKING FOR IT.

HENRY DAVID
THOREAU

I ALWAYS BELIEVE
I CAN BEAT THE BEST,
ACHIEVE THE BEST.
I ALWAYS SEE MYSELF
IN THE TOP POSITION.

SERENA WILLIAMS

I BELIEVE IN MYSELF,
EVEN MY MOST DELICATE
INTANGIBLE FEELINGS.

MARILYN MONROE

When
opportunity
knocks, open
the door

I OWE MY SUCCESS
TO HAVING LISTENED
RESPECTFULLY TO THE
VERY BEST ADVICE
AND THEN GOING AWAY
AND DOING THE EXACT
OPPOSITE.

G. K. CHESTERTON

**ALL PROGRESS
TAKES PLACE OUTSIDE
THE COMFORT ZONE.**

MICHAEL JOHN
BOBAK

It is confidence
in our bodies,
minds and spirits
that allows us to
keep looking for
new adventures.

OPRAH WINFREY

DON'T LET THE FEAR
OF LOSING BE GREATER
THAN THE EXCITEMENT
OF WINNING.

ROBERT KIYOSAKI

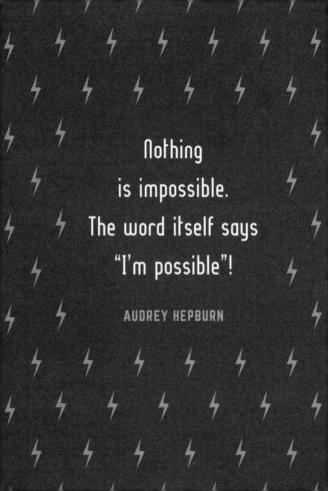

Nothing
is impossible.
The word itself says
"I'm possible"!

AUDREY HEPBURN

In order to succeed
we must first believe
that we can.

MICHAEL KORDA

**LUCK IS WHAT
HAPPENS WHEN
PREPARATION MEETS
OPPORTUNITY.**

SENECA

FAR AND AWAY THE BEST
PRIZE THAT LIFE HAS TO
OFFER IS THE CHANCE
TO WORK HARD AT WORK
WORTH DOING.

THEODORE ROOSEVELT

**POUR YOUR TIME
AND PASSION INTO
WHAT BRINGS YOU
THE MOST JOY.**

MARIE KONDO

THE TASK AHEAD IS NEVER GREATER THAN THE STRENGTH WITHIN YOU

I WILL WORK
IN MY OWN WAY,
ACCORDING TO
THE LIGHT THAT
IS IN ME.

LYDIA MARIA CHILD

YOU MISS
100 PER CENT OF
THE SHOTS YOU
DON'T TAKE.

WAYNE GRETZKY

If we could
change ourselves,
the tendencies
in the world would
also change.

MAHATMA GANDHI

ONE FINDS LIMITS
BY PUSHING THEM.

HERBERT A. SIMON

We are what we repeatedly do. Excellence, therefore, is not an act but a habit.

ANONYMOUS

Any transition is easier
if you believe in yourself
and your talent.

PRIYANKA CHOPRA

**SUCCESS IS OFTEN
ACHIEVED BY THOSE
WHO DON'T KNOW THAT
FAILURE IS INEVITABLE.**

COCO CHANEL

DREAM
BELIEVE
ACHIEVE

If you're interested in finding out more about our books, find us on Facebook at **Summersdale Publishers** and follow us on Twitter at **@Summersdale**.

www.summersdale.com